little eternities

Also by Sharon Chmielarz

Different Arrangements

But I Won't Go Out in a Boat

Stranger in Her House

The Other Mozart

The Rhubarb King

Calling

The Sky Is Great the Sky Is Blue

Love from the Yellowstone Trail

Visibility: Ten Miles
a Prairie Memoir in Photography and Poetry

The Widow's House

little eternities

poems

Sharon Chmielarz

NODIN PRESS

Cover photo: Sharon Chmielarz
Author Photo: Carol Lundquist
Design: John Toren

The *New Yorker* cartoon referred to across from section 1 page
appeared in the June 6 & 13, 2016 issue, p. 88.

The quotation from poet Bai Hua on page 40 appears in *Wind Says*,
page ix, translated by Fiona Sze-Lorrzin.

ISBN: 978-1-935666-99-8

Library of Congress Cataloging-in-Publication Data

Names: Chmielarz, Sharon, author.
Title: Little eternities : poems / Sharon Chmielarz.
Description: Minneapolis, MN : Nodin Press, [2017]
Identifiers: LCCN 2017031383 | ISBN 9781935666998
Classification: LCC PS3553.H57 A6 2017 | DDC 811/.54--dc23
LC record available at https://lccn.loc.gov/2017031383

Published by
Nodin Press, LLC
5114 Cedar Lake Road
Minneapolis, MN 55416

Printed in U.S.A.

To the imagination. To longing.

I

2

little eternities

"Time has always been the greatest wonder for me. Why is it now, but not then?"

— *Wind Says,* Bai Hua

"Time passes more slowly in that dimension, so take these sudokus."

— Cartoon caption by Edward Steed, *The New Yorker*

1

TIME TRAVELER

You are leaving
or arriving.
All the same
in deep time.

Paleolithic,
Pharaonic,
outer galactic
or old Gallic,

all the same
in deep time.

In your place
you are here
today.

You can film it,
you can pin it
down in ink,
you can try but

no one's seen it
like you've seen it.
I have seen you
in your jacket

once a robe
on an ancient
frieze in clay.

Summer of 2013

I was there. I always
wanted to live in 1913
and it came again,
a hundred years late,
but otherwise punctual
as a trombone slide
wandering slowly to
the accompaniment of
a brushed snare drum,
sh sh sh sh, feeling a bit
loose around the shoulders.
What time is

it anyway?—A train's
just pulled in, with
its chain of dark green
washed-to-gray *wagon lit*.
Diesel breath
fouls the station's air.
The groaning wheels
make it hard to hear
if someone's calling
to the young woman
in the train window.

Whether to the future or the past?

*

There's a yearning hovering
around like Russian roulette.

*

Now the young woman's slipping
on her good brown pumps.
Now she's sliding across the worn
plush bench and stands
in the train car's door.

From a notch of time
she surveys the platform's
crowd and then, nudged
by the minute and a passenger
behind her, she steps down.

If I Bend to Pick You Up

O! On my front stoop, hopping, a little sparrow.
Of all the birds in the world, you come to me, Sparrow.

You limp, you hobble. I can't help you though I want to;
I know nothing of fixing the flight of sparrows.

If my knees could bend, I'd scoop you up,
put you in a cardboard box, keep you safe, Sparrow.

You're just a sparrow after all, a common sparrow.
I'm not expected to take care of sparrows.

Your wing flutters, telling me what's wrong. I'm
the useless one. Physician, how do you heal a sparrow?

If he's to be mine after I unlock the front door,
he will be disappointed, whether man or sparrow.

Out of panic? fear? a last chance? you come so close
to my shoes, one-half inch more and—the tap of a sparrow.

Are you that humble to tap my foot?
Or does height mean nothing to a sparrow?

All I can offer is the shelter of my garden patch.
You retreat. I do not feel good about this, Sparrow.

Yes, stay there for tonight's storm, under the mugo pine.
Peck among seeds, the only food I have for sparrows.

Words may work on paper but they have the weight
of snow-grit which you may not see this year, Sparrow.

I'm so sorry. What if I die first? And death is so
untrustworthy. I, Sharon, could return as cat, Sparrow.

I Won't Turn on the Radio

rather I'll listen to the rain,
a rich companion promising
mutual benefits.

After a drought or long absence,
the god of rain can be steady
or scary. Chaque/ Tlaloc to the South.

Thor's thunder from the North.
I love them both. Some nights
love can be desperate

as well as passing.
Mine bears no grudges
against rain's music,

its artful way in bed
leading the listener
to sleep's side.

In an Armchair, Timeless,

liking the sudden
movement of beyond
the window where birds
fly by, where movement
comes to go away, not knowing
gone is a word for everything seen.
                                    Drifting,

seeing *again*—Geese this time. Seeing
gone. Quiet = gone. Sensing *here*.
Sensing *there* light has moved.
Something has shifted. No
word for *I* but *I* very
present. Also, *I am*.

                    Drifting,
not knowing *I am* is a name.
Possibly knowing possession, the way
light possesses when it catches the eye.

FRAGMENTS FROM A POLISH JOURNAL, *1889*

Berlin. *Wien.* London. Money can be

     a gleaming avenue, a night

of snow, a fine dizzying swirl, a cold

     white wine's kind of spin under

the street lamp where I catch up with him.

His coat's wool, wet with snow. My thoughts,

     reined in, bolt in places

of their own choosing. Would I trade

     my house for his?

 I hold him tightly around the waist.

This morning, hoarfrost. The Vistula's

     waves like icy fish tails.

My days?—A tight-fitting shoe whose heel

     snaps on a cobble, then

the detestable limp home.

Come back, *Kochanie*, see if your lips

     still suit the curve in my hand.

SIZE

I was in a dress shop that ranked sizes 3 to 0,
    0 being a size where even robins
loom large, where the rest of the world is

a snow field 0-woman slogs through daily, taking
    her small heart in tow, whispering
to it, "Courage, courage," the way the French

pronounce a singingly low-pitched chocolaty vowel—
    ahzh!—which soothes
the size-rage a small American may feel. A petty

thought if the 0-woman is a black belt in Karate
    or a Sunday schooler
or Yeshiva student studying David and Goliath,

or *Small Is Beautiful* like social justice Catholics,
    though that never was
as successful in Guatemala as "Black Is Beautiful"

in Chicago and was subsumed in the early 21st century
    by Hummer-like Big Business
and rashes of heartlessness. Remember *The Glass*

Menagerie, those frail figures, how they crouched
    when Jim entered the room?
Their only chance to hide away was to be over-

looked, to never ask a total stranger for a kiss
    out of loneliness in a city
of complications so beyond miniature it's more

like a minotaur heart devourer. Everything
       snaps when the heart
is swallowed or must be squirreled away

like the family silver from invaders. 'Heartless'
       can burn like a million
tiny red hearts on 0-woman's javelin.

EYE HOLE (EAGPYREL = EYE)

Not to be confused with window, the wind's eye. So many
scenes pass by. Look what we walk through! An image climbs
in and then climbs out, followed by galloping thought. Only
a film maker can keep up. At the wedding dance, how it felt
to have the skirt blooming at thigh level. And how it felt to
move in close to the other's chest. This may feel so good
you close your eyes. The eye hole can't feel like your arms
and breasts; its god-like power is limited, demanding light,
blinking at darkness, maybe even threatened by it, scared by
the thought of non-existence. How long did life on earth
have to wait before eye holes evolved? Some priest somewhere
knows exactly within ten thousand years.

A compromise on
dress straps ended the cold war between one priest and a
bride. You see, her bridesmaids' dresses, cranberry-colored
with a black ribbon for a belt, were strapless. Not whorish,
in spite of the priest's insistence the shoulders be covered.
His nose holes, a-flare; wrath inside those hairy tunnels. Oh,
bosoms! Some eyes like to follow you, finding silhouettes
and full fronts beautiful and sexy, and others want you hidden under dishtowels. Consider how old this conflict is.
1500 years ago the word for 'eye' was *eagpyrel*. How long
before that did we wait before we could see blindness? An
eye doesn't know. Still, it's so valuable it comes with its own
protective lid. Well. This is how eternity works, so far.—
Swallows rise and fly, dip in and out of a cliff's craters that
look very much like the dark eye holes in Argus's skull.

SEE

Such a perfectly shaped word
in sound and effect: *See.*
As if you were standing
on a rise, overlooking the floor
of a valley. And despite the wind
in your eyelashes, you can clearly
see a combine down there threshing. *See*

works just as well on a calm
day spent not on a ridge
but anywhere the eyes narrow
when discovering a particularly
difficult insight.

THISTLE

In summer they take their places in the field,
a small happy down-doing that changes
in autumn, a session of ride-out-the-bother,
thorny, prickly as a sharp upper lip. Many
days, like 253, 879, are thistles under your
proverbial saddle. No one sees them, just as
no one sees thistles (or nettles) nap. No one is
embarrassed for them. They're thirty-three
million years old, and their name—thistle,
Distel—is 368,000 years old. Etymologists
have searched through twelve hundred years
of words to find the origin and so far, no luck.
If you eat the bull thistles' blooms when
they're silky dark purple in the field or
crowding the pasture's fence, they taste like
candy, magic, and valor returning each year
while standing still.

THE DOMINANCE OF PUMPKIN
OVER FIELD AND IMAGINATION

In crack and split. In thump thump beat.
In a mighty vine's sluice to fruit. In seed,
white almond eyes or lids, roasted in an oven
on the way to heaven in solidarity with the moon.

Humans want their gods to look like them
and lead them through the dark – a way of holding
winter off, a way celery stalks cannot, nor
all the skins in onion, or the rootedness

of underground carrot, beet, and parsnip.
When cut open and done, pumpkin becomes
summer's sacrifice. All that's left behind is
roundness and triangle and a darkly cheery face.

some numbers are so old they were first
counted on thumbs, long before humans
described numbers with names and pinned
one's solitary status down, in times when
the potter in his hut never went beyond
a surplus of two. Demands for more
yielded stick markings in the yard's dirt
to show 'how much.' And maybe nouns
stepped in, the equivalent of our own
"a lot," "a bunch."—"How many warriors?"
"As many as the villagers in the valley."
Accumulation wanted exactness though.
Beyond ten, fingers struggled with the weight
to be more than a bone-creaking abacas;
hands, more than a carousel of counting.
The brainy wanted squaring and pairing
and leapt figuratively from the first knuckle
toward the mind's imagined pi—All the while
that old, lovely chaos, Zero in her room,
rocking in her chair, held her offsprings'
feet to the *ur* deca-system, the original frame.

On Time

I really should fix my clock. This morning when I roll over to check the time I see it's 7:53 which yesterday would mean 6:53. Then I notice there's only one little green dot in the upper corner on the clock face which means it has automatically left God's time and it really is 7:53. Or in this case, it's 7:38 since the clock runs 15 minutes fast and four months slow.

I hate to tinker with things. Look for their instructions. Read them. Fiddle around with buttons and what-nots. That's what I like about wind-up clocks: their goings on are much easier to figure out. Mine's a preference for easy times over hard times.

Although if Father Time poised his scythe over your neck, I'm the kind who'd try hard to save you in time.

Since November and up to yesterday I've had some good times with this clock facing my pillow. Coming out of sleep's halls, I've had a whole hour to myself before the world's time schedule began. A whole hour awake in spacey timelessness.

Today that's changed. I'm behind before I'm even up. Like the God of Old, the clock with the one green eye means business. It is what it is when it's all by itself. 8:30 is 8:30. I don't like it. Time and the bed have become unfriendly neighbors. Time's pulled on its pants and slid into its shoes. It's running without waiting to see if I can catch up. I have no time to stop and fix this clock.

A WHITE ROSE WOULD DO FOR
ALL MY TROUBLES

A trip to your dock, van Gogh, would do,
or a stroll into your sky. Let me lie
on your narrow bed or sit in the corner

chair. Don't be home because, dude,
the truth is you sort of scare me.
Gimme an antidote. I'll leave you

some money on the table. I am
what your brother might call desperate,
what you might paint as a solitary tree

where by all rights there shouldn't be a tree.

On Milton's Political Pamphlets and the Measure of Time

"London, Printed by Mathew Simmons, next dore to the gilded Lyon in Aldersgate Street, 1649."

As if the gilded *Lyon* would always be next *dore*,
ready to direct a writer's steps to the ancestor
of photocopiers near Aldersgate's homely glamour—
a fading *Lyon*. (A sign above a pub's door?
A statue, its *gilt* fading?) The present is so
strong in its little day-by-day affairs, bringing
down its lions somedays seems impossible.
Simmon's client Milton, for example, hiding
on a straw bed of fleas under a common, stale
coverlet.—Oh, a republic had seemed so
possible, buoyed on the stream of his pamphlets
arguing against a monarch's so-called sacred
calling. It seemed the civil war had ended
the dispute as if it wouldn't recur, in England
or elsewhere. As if *dore* could never be
spelled *door*. As if life couldn't be summed up
as an immense series of changing cruelties,
preserving, somewhat, a tittle of civility:
for appearance sake Milton's Parlimentarians
sewed King Charles's chopped-off head
back on for one last public display. (Using
horse hair or wire for thread?) But
the inscrutable *That Is* intrudes. Charles II
ascends the throne and Milton goes underground.
Try understanding this when the world's in upheaval,
and you have only a bit of lead to hold onto—
oh, the printer's clever fingers—one bit
for each letter in a word that, heavens! stays put.

ONCE

A pitiless word, weighing time in its slight
hand. Once and for all.

The prince's kingdom the king surrendered.
The parking lot, once a horse meadow.

He could have been a somebody, could
have had class. Once she was beautiful,

everyone danced upon a time. You used
to live here once. We were happy. I knew you.

I loved you. Once.

To Time and Its Progress

four scenes

through catacomb alleys of claustrophobia
in a hillside city, all nine hundred years
of it, time gets lost, lets the donkey
trot by—*Balak! Balak!*—mixes fate
in the souk with an ancient scent:

donkey dung, nougat, bloody slabs
of beef, cedar chips, dates and fine wool
djellabas, saffron, leather dyed in vats,
brown, yellow, orange, blue for purses
and their foreign, Freudian interpretations.

Muted now, in a more recent century,
time gleams in the hotel's floor tiles.
The bar–serving mint tea, too—
and lobby's armchairs face a wall
of windows. Time can rest here

in your body all afternoon. Wearing
a black suit a server more polite than
anyone you know, offers with a bow
whatever year you desire. With or
without sugar, he asks, wielding his tray.

≈

An olive tree
        from the 15th century—
                the village's main attraction—

is inhabited by a cat who may be
        a reincarnation on a limb, hearing
                the call to prayer

dissipate over the souk,
        over houses and gravestones
                painted blue for protection

from demons. *There is no god but Allah*
        say the needles of school girls,
                say the old and young men,

the faithful in the souk, sewing wool and
        linen *djellabas* as donkeys trot by,
                their cargo, empty propane cans

knocking against their scrawny ribs.
        Listen–a Peugeot starts, purring
                in the rain. A toaster-

sized radiator in the hotel room
        gurgles thin heat.
                (Thank you. *Shukran*)

A cat caterwauls in an alley.
        A little girl with a pink umbrella,
                pink purse and book bag, sloshes by.

It's Friday, baking day for the town's
        oven, a small white room
                in its own quiet corner.

A man stands at the oven's door
        pushing a bread board in
                and out comes the village bread.

                ≈

The last of the sun's rays catches a herd
of black goats, bleating on a sand dune's ridge.

They *wedel* like skiers down the slope into
the Touregs' camp. Then it's night, beetle black.

The easy stars come out first. The easily
identified: Orion. The Big Dipper.
The air is cool after heat, what it means
to live in desert silence without shelter.

The stars' explosions burst belly to belly
until there's no room for one star more.
Like any dark reptile on the sand
all of me is in my eyes, glittering.

≈

Outside a window in Sultan Bayezid's herbal room,
the garden's still May in the fifteenth century,
his peonies blush pink, the roses, red.

The room is cool as marble against a cheek,
calm as lute music and the clopping rhythm of horse
and wagon in the street. The driver's head glides along

above the garden wall. In an empire of pointed shoes
and caftans, music and gardens are the prescription
for the depressed, the melancholic, the dark-eyed psychotic,

the epileptic, the catatonic. The man in the foyer
asks for a rose; another patient, just standing
in the hall, eyes vacant, holds a carnation

against a world of male malady. A woman lies
on the door bench as if stabbed. I turn away. Oh, knots
and twists of a different sort, I belong to you.

SUMMER

Sommer, *Sommar*, summer is a coming-in from the pre Indo-European word meaning "fly" as in gnats as well as "fly" in *tempus fugit*, a late-comer upstart from *Roma* where wolves raised barbarian boys on the banks of the Tiber. *Basta*. It's summer. Again. And my sister is busy killing flies in her back yard. Our Father couldn't stand a fly either, coming as he did from the farm where everything humans do behind a door or bush is revealed by animals and insects in the open. Because indoors flies crawl over food on their teeny, offal-speckled legs, not one fly survived in our house. The swatter's location was burned into my sisters' and my brains, home-made like the swatter since the Governor never bought anything he could make himself. His was a floppy swatch of window screen on a wire handle doubled for strength. It gave the fly a huge advantage, impossible as it was to hit any fly head-on with it. Mother usually cheated, preferring a rolled-up section of the *Reminder* for the wallop. Slowly I strayed over to her side. Many summers passed, swatting. Walking home alone from the show hall at night, I confess, I the Tween used to peep into neighbors' windows from the sidewalk to see how others lived, my thoughts crawling over their dusty screens in search of—swat, the shade flipped down. One more fly plastered to night's sticky ceiling. Well, *tempus fugit* as do places, people, fly swatters, emotions and nostalgia too, tomatoes and zinnias and flicks with good endings.

A LIFE WITH THE MOVIES

Not too much, is it, to ask from a week—
Tuesday. *Night of the Iguana*. Tequila.
I'd hate to drink to nothing at all.

Wednesday, *The Northwest Passage* to Friday,
I lift my glass to the empty chair beside me.
Not too much, is it? To ask from a week?

Thursday is totally *Mutiny on the Bounty*.
I mix a *Titanic*: drink three and you're sunk.
I'd hate to drink nothing at all.

Chicago. Valentine's Day. Al Capone. Still
bloody alone. Calls for a double shot.
Not too much to ask from a week. Is it

Saturday? *Dinner at Eight*. 1933. I'm late.
Sunday's *Love in the Afternoon* is a boring fling.
I hate to drink to nothing. After all

Father Knows Best. Monday is a light white
wine, sipped for all the *Miss Lonely Hearts*.
Not too much to ask, is it, from a week
of drinking to nothing at all? That I'd hate.

BILGE

... nasty, cruddy, nothing you'd want to drink during
Happy Hour to get high or "blue," as the Germans say,
blau, floating over the waves of Dead Drunk Away!
And on the dry shore, on New Year's Eve, the *feme sole*'s
drama in the living room as she waits for her sweetheart to
stumble home from the office. Hers is a heart, my friends,
that clings to dregs. Where are you, dear Lover of the fat,
the crippled, the pimpled, the epileptic, the bilge? Step
up to the bar. Is it your leg straining against mine? O,
Dishwater Blond Stranger. Can I hope you care?

SLEEK

—the grasses
standing tinder dry
and dun, running in wind
toward the tracks, toward the scrawny
border of gravel between steel
rails and thin stems

—the snow
whirling outside
the window while
the absinthe level in the bottle
sinks, and a wife on a chrome
bar stool whirls and pulls her
pursestrings ever tighter

—a season,
any season,
passing by,
a black locomotive
ramming through the night's
starry noose

—the white horse
racing beside it

L'Arlésienne: Madame Joseph-Michel Ginoux, Van Gogh, 1888-89

"These hard features were once soft, and these cold, almost malicious eyes were friendly and innocent."
— Robert Walser, *Looking at Pictures*

But she is pretty, Herr Walser. Look again.
You don't like the single line that leads
at the same time up to a curved eyebrow
and down to rosebud lips? Or her 1920
movie star posture at the table, resting
her cheek on her big hand, a useful hand
that's seen its share of gutting geese
and dusting off a book? She may stumble
over a word, back up and start again
but she can read.
        Maybe, Herr Walser,
you misjudged the ambition in her eyes?
She's happily obliged to wear her best,
her Sunday dress, a navy with a pale
green scarf. She's primped a bit combing
her dark satiny hair. She's wet her fingers
to set her bangs in spit curls. Just so
on the forehead. And pat into place a navy
matron's cap with scarf-tail. Just so

she sits in the painting for hours, years,
never hearing a demand for tea or lunch.
She's busy dreaming, Herr Walser,
on a week day no less, dreaming herself
into Madame L'Arlésienne who's seen
the world outside of Arles: Each morning
in Paris she heard a bright scale of tones,
Bonjour, Madame. Bonjour, Madame.
The souvenir welcomes her to all the time
in the world, even to herself at the table
with three books, one open, two waiting.

THE TSARINA'S TEA SET

Museum of Russian Art, Minneapolis

Incredible the Bolsheviks didn't smash it,
token of the Tsarina and the wild-eyed
Rasputin, who accidentally on purpose could've
ground a porcelain cup in his teeth
and not bled, proving to her his powers,

grinning and chomping down the delicate
painted birds on the cup, its background
a robin's egg blue or the tint in a woman's
bedroom wallpaper.—Swallow-like birds
I can't name, their own invincible magic

flown from a brush's dash-dash, o,
trickle-down, tangible happiness, the royal
that escaped assassination. O happy little
birds, happy blue teapot boxed in a museum's
vitrine. You'll be the family that lasts forever.

BUMBLE

So here you sit, if you're still alive and reading through old journals. If you're dead, hello to anyone else reading this. It's September, the air, still; a breeze barely tousles shadows. The light, its own sheer curtain, fills the window. In twenty years hence, now will be as lost to you as today's flowers, a rusted yellow so striking the vase's black band glows. It matches the dishes bought decades ago at Anderson's. Homey reminders via a Finnish crockery factory of the many years since. You probably still pretend your lover just walked in the door aiming the weekly bouquet at your heart. You've always been good at arranging facts to your taste. Second attempts at personal failures can be found in yesterday's papers and obituaries: *Today would have been 19 years ... Until we see each other again.* The great hope, to be together again, and this time there'd be no bumbling.—Not the strangest thing you and I have known to happen.

PUMMEL

As in pummeling the doubly wobbly, whopping the rumps against a wall, great thumps, first the right and then the left; trim that posterior down to slim slim. Strip the word of any upper class. Tush, bum, butt, tail, buttocks, gluts, rear end, fanny, bottom, arse. Ladies, shiver behind your fans, you have one, too, dumpy compared to the head with its abundance of holes. *O, my.* In the upper and out the nether. O.

Big cheeks don't feel at home on a sunny day when the slim sports crowd is feeling happy, and their pleasure is catchy. But great when angry and snarling, *Get your A___ out of here.* As if it were its own cart, a piece of objectionable, unwanted equipment. Sensitive antennae pick up on this quickly. But the ass can be a beauty for a roll in the hay; big hips something to grip and hold onto as the willy sinks in. Ah, great pleasure in that spongy peach and perch. When we die we'll be remembered for our good side.

The 900 Pound Man, the Fattest in the World

He did not wear shoes, had no shoes,
for no shoes fit his monstrous feet
or held his monstrous weight. And besides
he didn't need shoes in bed.
                          Nor do
caterpillars in their cocoons, devouring
every hour on their way to butterfly (while he ate
he felt so light).
                          He did not wear pants,
such as we know pants. His were sheets, sewn
half way up the middle? And for a shirt,
a third sheet cut like a poncho?
                          Who

could gather him in her arms, who
could get close enough to meet his lips,
drawn and thin—
                          His eating

was a longing to stop time?—He lost

six hundred pounds, had to pick up
his loose flesh to walk or shove a leg
into pants. A chattering pack of hounds,
blue-gloved nurses and surgeons with

scalpels, met at his borders and filleted
away bags full of flesh, saving
the capillaries, bloody little
creeks running right under
the epidermis, peripheries
he must not lose.

                          To think

the 900 pound man ate farther into
oblivion than any human ever
on this planet. His weight the little
country he made for himself.

THE WOUNDED ANGEL

painting, Hugo Simberg, 1903

This happened long ago when blood
root bloomed, the dazed spring still
holding onto makeshift railings.

We sloshed around winter's old fields
in poor man's shoes, bought large
to grow into. We heard the stubble

breathe, *caution, caution,* saw
something white crumple and fall
from the sky. A heron? Wild swan?

We ran toward it. A wingéd thing,
a heap of feathers we carried home,
her feet too odd for any shoes.

That was the year an angel lived
in our kitchen, recuperating
on the bench beside Mother's oven.

She isn't like us, Mother said,
when we're tired or hurt.
She won't put up any fuss.

That was the year we learned
about earth and its gravities,
how they hold some of us

down, but free the unearthly.
From the kitchen's back stoop
we three watched the angel

unfurl her wings one morning
and barefoot, take flight
into the blue, infinite sky.

FYRD

This word moves like a year repeating itself, her
skinny hand, clutching mine. She, the keeper
of stuff. *Give it all away,* she chortles, *what was
fun was missing the boat, I done it often enough.*
As if it were all of this and all that in a sack of
skins, something to be buried, old. Old always
looks alike when the house shades block out light.

—No one understands you any more, I tell her, but
fyrd doesn't care.

2

"That rose, like all roses, only bloomed for one morning."
– Balzac

"That summer, like all summers, only bloomed for one life."
– Bai Hua

MAGELLAN

I made the acquaintance of Magellan today.
He was navigating the den's beige carpet,
heading from south southwest toward north
on a steady, almost lethargic course, his leggy
arms oaring first on his right, then left. No
Southern Cross or helpful wind to guide him
over the nap's waves and dangerous shoals.
Luckily the overcast ceiling kept an albatross
from picking him off. I left him to his odyssey
exploring the ocean I can walk.
                                        Hours later
and two feet, or two thousand strokes from
the bookcase shore, I found Magellan lying
belly-up, his goal capsized. No kin showed
to carry him off or eat his carapace, an oval,
the softness of dust and wither in brown books.
He was light, an advantage for torpid steering
on a soundless solo-voyage to wherever-after.
Some humans ask nothing from no thing, too,
and walk off alone into extremes—the heat of
memory, ice or mist or barn–till no longer seen.

A STRANGE FALLING

"We've decided to go on living."
　　　　– Robert Falcon Scott, expedition to the South Pole, 1912

They decide, council style, huddled in the wind-
　　　　whipped tent. A nod from each man.
Not like a personal fiat whispered into a pillow
　　　　after a night's struggle with a "new
reality" when the mind offers the choice of going on, or not.

The thirty ponies, already dead. The men, half human,
　　　　half horse, must pick up the slack,
yoked to the sleds, and pull a thousand pounds of dead
　　　　weight and an extra thirty-five pounds of
rocks collected as they work their way toward the South

Pole, their courtesan, the favorite one. Serious men,
　　　　frigging fools, some say, in mourning
for the friend who's run to his quick, bare death naked.
　　　　They spend two hours wrapping their toes
before they pull on their socks. They'll want toes

when they return to England, to groups of intimate
　　　　friends who'll gather around the rocks
found by five famished men famous for being the first
　　　　to come across the Norwegian flag
snapping claim to the Pole. And they, among the most

disappointed of men on earth that day, decide to keep
　　　　dragging the sleds toward a more distant
death, perhaps in England. Theirs, unlike the tinier,
　　　　undramatic fraction of pluck offered
from warm bed covers to go on under the falling All.

STARRY NIGHTS OF PANTRY LABOR

"I was born very far from where I'm supposed to be,
so I'm on my way home."

– Bob Dylan

Maybe soulscape begins as door.
        Your hand, hesitant on the handle,

not sure where you'll feel at home.
        Yours won't come looking for you.

A sea rushes in only so far. Deserts demand
        you stumble onto them.

The search is a little like flirting, like
        the flirting between Jesus

and the Samaritan woman at the well,
        her oasis in an arid land

where they prattled on, each sharing
        their thoughts on water.

Sometimes you follow the harsh back
        of winter to find the scape

that matches you. It may happen
        on a starry night of pantry labor:

what is missing, what is at hand.
        Light streams in, wave after wave

moves through your rooms,
        your traversable mountains.

A SMALL REPAST OF TEA AND KIPPERS

One day I shall swim away like a herring,
he said.
And be eaten like a fish by death,
she said.
At high tea, high tide; she
pours, he divides the fish.

She asked what was that noise
outside.
He thought it a loose shingle,
flapping.
They both heard his belly,
growling. Later, the sea

calmed down. Murmured, she said.

In Praise of Pencils

1.

An ordinary history includes ancestors
and their entourage; for a pencil, the first
sharpeners, a jack knife, a butcher knife.
Chippers, nickers. Later the screw-like
rig housed in a metal box, the pencil's
tip held straight to the task while a rear
end wiggled and a hand cranked.
A sharp pencil has everything to do
with books: clear notes in margins.
In small histories December evenings
may be spent in a book store though
the night outside be cold and dark.

2.

If there's a shortage of money or a surplus
of martyrdom, one puts up with dullness.

It isn't morbid to consider the time left. Is it
to be spent writing with a stub?

Present time offers pencils honed
by electric sharpeners, a real mark

of progress. The same fragrance
escapes the lead. The same woodsy

pine. The hope chest cedar. A pointy
graphite solitude, a tiny mountain peak,

sable black. When pressed not too hard,
not too lightly to paper, it talks.

THESE OLD WOMEN

These old women in the woods of Poland
or Babel's stories—they knew nothing.
What books had they read? What operas
heard? Philosophers?—Unknown to them.
Their beds were their dearest distractions.
I neither admire nor envy them.
Troublemakers. Bedrock. Soup makers.
Swallowers of all they'd been given.
Deliverers acquainted with habits of
children, of love, lust, the Holy Ghost
of seasons, the first steps toward death—
so startling when they were girls.
One step led, as they learned, to the next.

LOVE FOR OLD PLACES PEOPLED BY PEOPLE LIKE ME

that is, one-half wanting to return under
cover to beginnings, the other knowing

returned, we'd be foreign.

This tug of war. Have you stood
in the middle of night's dark fevers

knowing the child called up to the Front?

On those evenings when light filters
through house windows, west windows,

the house becomes a necessary union.

SMALL ALRIGHT

To small, really small, a needle's eye is a boastful giant. Just about as big as an ant. Nothing makes me squirm more than the thought of an ant in bed crawling over my open lips. Well, a worm would be worse. But then you're getting into something bigger than a small itch, something in plain sight, like getting an A on your second grade worksheet for All Right. No mistakes. What a high. You don't forget the beautiful red A, not rounded but straight-sided, not crawling over your name but propping it up in the top right-hand corner. Two red poles linked by a very small bar.

SHIT

My mother used it as an expletive over fleshy, unwanted surprises. *Sotto voce*, dismissing any diktat to keep the mouth's temple pure. Pretty soon I was using it, too. Father preferred son-of-a-bitch and a goddammit that froze the air in any room. I never heard him say *shit* though. Shit wasn't bad enough. Not mean and disgusted enough. For shit's truly ancient. The Neanderthals for sure had it in their vocabulary. "Go out and collect some shit-pies for the fire." "Look. A pile of auroch shit. Get your club ready." And stink? I don't think they objected. To defecate meant you ate. You'd stay alive. Alive was better than dead. Alive was kind of holy. As are etymology's trips into the past. Shit is a direct relative of *Scheiss* which in German isn't one of the seven taboo words. What's the big deal? We make it. If the colon's working we deal with it naturally. But if you want to sound really bothered, say *Scheissdreck*. Now there's a word to clear out the cheeks. Say that while chewing flaky boiled cauliflower and you've got a real mess on your plate. It shows what you think of the world.

FOR THE MILLIONS WHO WERE STARVED TO DEATH IN UKRAINE

the Holodomor, man-made famine, 1932-33

In the Lands of Et Cetera and the recurring Et Al where
genocides come and go, will be and have been, ordered on
a timetable by the emperor of madness,
                              a footpath
through a field leads to the hollow where a body
collapsed and its life passed, a life that in the afterwards
continues in saved letters and rumors
         "... have sent to Poland all the clothes
we could sell for food."
         She ate her baby? –He would've died anyway.
         "...and a man cannot endure this for a long time.
There are eight in our family..."
                              The clothes chest, empty.
The grass, picked clean. Insects and birds, long ago eaten.

IRON

All those iron hearts Christ warned would do themselves in,
or was it the god in Psalms, calling his children hard-hearted
and stubborn? Their iron shrugs, iron groans, iron-clad alibis,
iron masks. No traits of his own of course: his are wings and
light weather at its best, mysterious in its lack of ambition,
His is routine, a gentle shadowing across the lawn, the extra
pump in a heartbeat. It's possible to find a sigh in iron then.

POSTCARD TO MR. MIŁOSZ

"Aï, my dead of long ago! Aï,Hanusevich, aï, Nina!
Nobody remembers you, nobody knows about you ....
He (Mister Hanusevich) caroused with chanteuses, pretending to be
a big shot,
Would send a telegram in Russian, 'Arriving with ladies
Meet with music troikas champagne ...'
And a signature: Count Bobrinskii."

> – from "Mister Hanusevich" by Czesław Miłosz

I was there, too, though I am here. I'm the good girl, was
the good girl in the back of the restaurant by the door. I
volunteer to tell how you pulled on your brown leather
jacket, sleeve by slippery satin-lined sleeve, how the evening was classy, arrogant, expensive, how the big bill waved
unpaid in Uncle Innkeeper's hand as we left, laughing,
waiting for the troika that came late. (Nina's patent leather
shoes got soaked.) That night was like all nights staked out
for us. Though I wasn't there, I am here in a nerdy, literary
twist on the Ruthian promise *Wherever you go, I will go,*
following Mr. Hanusevich, et al, all bedfellows on paper,
midge-y shadows that bugged your hand, tagged along as
you write. Wrote. It's questionable you'll ever read this,
lying as your body does in a crypt on a familiar Kraków
street. Who knows. But you made that night, like all
nights, bloom for the spangle-hatted and gutsy, the great
pretenders, the big-shot high rollers, the champion champagne cork poppers, the Count Bobrinskiis of the confis-
cated country estates, the most boozy of angels.

p.s. I love how you shrug, so your jacket: or a phrase: fits:
hangs: right.

PHOTO: EARLY 1930's, BERLIN, A MAN DANCING WITH A WOMAN

Berliners are good at brushing aside worrisome
weekday thoughts on Sunday afternoons, strange
preparations, little last minute storehouses of charm
and fun at dance halls along the Kurfürstendamm.

And that whirling couple?—Doing it for sure
with clothes on. Zest blitzes from his shoes to her
chic pumps. Naked pleasure, though she's covered
her hair with a hat. She has no eyes for the future,

yet she follows, chin on his shoulder, the course
they're taking toward the door. It could get worse—
if the brown shirt interrupts their spinning past
his table. For now he's busy knocking back his thirst.

BIG

... hand pushing your head
down like an unweaned
kitten's into the milk
bowl, holding you
there, *drink or drown,*
until you catch on.

HAPPINESS

He hadn't been drinking, not for a Long Time, but things were very very and she feared a slip and the puzzling remarks on the radio that morning, a man parsing genes like a tax collector, 40% you're stuck with, 60% can go either way. Not to forget chemical imbalances that may seem joyful but leave a person sad and angry and frustrated, ravines her mind wandered, courting easier, distracting thoughts: quarrels with friends, grocery store lists. When suddenly there he was, in the kitchen on the stool, feeling, well OK, *looking* miserable. Head down, chin on his chest, he quietly said he wanted to go to hell. Happiness, the radio had said, is mostly found in small daily instances with occasional, merely occasional, mind you, spurts of great joy. But what about the nameless and faceless times, the random solitary hours, the body of bones rattling through empty rooms once renown for light glossing the windows, sofa, chair, table, bookcase, turning everything into a creature of light, alive and glowing. Wordless. And slowly she felt, yes, she should say it, acknowledge it, a kind of coo-coo pleasure. Possibly a spurt.

CITY OF ARHIRIT

1976, James Turrell

Was it founded to be happy,
somewhere in Morocco,
or maybe Spain?

Perspective
leads past a street
corner to the narrow

hall all old lanes
turn into.
At the end, light

makes a red border
around a closed door.
The air

is so dense
breathing turns
into midnight.

BUTCHER

Must be an old one out there in the shed. His hands
shake as he slits the sow's throat, *press in, slash, release*
much like a heart beat gone berserk from booze or
overwork on a hot day.

(In the family of butchers: surgeons, magician knife-
wielders, pirates. Sculptors. Once, barbers. And the non-
union woman chopping up a chicken for Sunday dinner.)

And it is sweltering hot out in the shed and in the work
dividing fat from flesh, flesh from blood. Then you got
the hide, the bones, more fat, the guts, the sweetmeats
to render and process. The butcher wipes his dripping
forehead with his sleeve, flops his cap back on again.

Now his pails are full. Flabby chunks of flesh. He knows
a pig from inside out. Always chuckles about that. Mid-
morning the kid and his motorcycle will roar into the yard.
He'll fill the saddlebags with flesh. Slide the liver into its
own plastic bag, a quivering sack of blood. Liver is specialty
at the town square's market. Fresh for some woman's
noon table.

Mumbling. The butcher's almost knocked over a bucket.
What a mess that would be. And no blood left for purply
blood sausage.

For sure there's more to life than butchering. Though
eventually along comes his appetite for the wife's Sunday
pork roast.

An Afternoon Spent Reading
Madame Bovary

The pages are so dry they've turned tea brown.
They match the light, no stronger than a candle's

this dark afternoon. I discover *Madame Bovary*
and I grew up in the same peasant frugality,

a dream-slayer that keeps a romantic in check.
Flaubert noticed this type and wondered

what would happen if a woman let loose.
I look up from the page to listen: it's

pouring; under siege the roof sounds sturdy,
a Flaubert roof, all joints fit together as soundly

as the plot doing Mme Bovary in. Slowly
she sinks with me into my safe, paid-for chair.

And now wind howls around my front door;
the window tree wrestles an invisible opponent.

Is Bovary born as example of girlish passion
and innocent profligacy? Both exits for her,

the housebroken. As was death.—And Flaubert
the Omniscient, the Stalker follows her

to that end. "...the silence, the night,
the passing wind, the damp odors rising

from the ground." (p. 243) From the chair
comes the scratch of another page turned.

The Village Bakery

is open every day of the year
except Wednesdays and holy days,
and Saturdays after wedding days,
windy days and weak-kneed days,
days of travail, wholly incomprehensible
days of obligation, days of heaven
and hell, birthdays and name days, blue
days, paydays, anniversary days, days
of failed leaven, days of being otherwise
sleep-encamped days, days after
love-making day, dazed days, split-
hair days and lost key days, ruined
and lackadaisical days, mouse-turds-
in-the-flour days, days when the Lord
Himself says, *Better bar the door.*

CHAPEL ON THE MOUNTAIN

I'm the wide, white sweep of a cape
upon a mountain. At the end
of a pilgrim's path, the belly
you enter to sing, my feet buried
in the mountain's bed of boulders.
I tell you my shoulders
thrill to the wash of currents
from church bells and wind.
Look. A man in black, in silhouette,
hurries toward me, his shirt tails flying.

Van Gogh Appears at the Café Amoré

No chairs fly through the air tonight,
no linseed oil drips from a homemade brush,
no argument ensues over process,
for Gauguin does not appear,

just Vincent, or a dead ringer for him,
sitting alone, off the sauce, buzzing
on straight coffee and surrounded by
photos of flowers and dogs, pretty

but dead without the van Gogh dash
of madness, burned ego & desire
to be the god of the least bud: Bloom!
And then a young woman joins him,

runs a glance over his yellow denim
jacket, his unkempt hair, ruddy red,
his cheek's stubble shadow, in silhouette
Vincent was always at his best.

She's as beautiful as a buxom sonnet,
as a sunflower or olive tree tattoo.
After an hour together he wants to do her,
but she leaves alone, leaves him to spend

the rest of the evening in his room, not
the first sting he's pried out of his skin
by distracting himself with color,
or stars, or nights, or wild imperious air.

The Fetchers

" ...35,000 year-old-flute made of mammoth tusk found
in Germany."

a flute created from an idea
                        found while fooling around
(blowing through a hollow reed)
                        sturdier though, carved from tusk

made lithesome by chiseling
                        the mammoth's weapon–its fork
and threat, its wagging glower,
                        its *do-not-come-close.*

Add the chiseler's patience.
                        Add the whatever progenitor
to modern drill, a gadget gauging
                        out solid animal worry. A tool

turned to music.—From the same
                        boggy spots eons later rose
Bach, Beethoven in flesh and blood
                        and music. Here you may come close.

LOAD

Cheers to the load of wonderfully old words scattered from a crate that split open in a bardic library centuries ago and rolled into mouse holes, were swept up into bins or got stuck on the dustiest of back shelves. Along came Anatoly Lieberman, that up-loaded off-loaded down-loaded dude who tenderly collects them and their family histories. Words like *mickle little idle nimble brittle.* This morning a moving event reminds me of the difficulty and joy in his work: A semi hauling pigs overturned on 35W south. Pigs out of the poke. Pigs loose and squealing on that freeway. Pigs named 'pig' since before 1225. (Think wattle. Woodenware. Pegs. Mead. Brute force.) These pigs stopped traffic. Squad cars blinked blue-red, red-blue. Coppers, truck driver, commuters chased down slippery sows and hogs like metaphors. Across lanes they ran, onto the shoulder and into ditches. SU-EY! *Midge-girl-mugger-crab-tooth-clover-slop-north-ransack-knuckle-tune. SU-EY!* Their music makes a day worth living. (Poor pigs.)

On Infusion

Infusion, that popular word at the bar—
lavender in a martini, cucumber in vodka—
hasn't described (until now?) the Annunciation,
the Angel Gabriel trembling before the Virgin
Mary so tender and mild and fluttering his wings
about her, equal in grandeur to any Grecian
god impregnating a mortal with the future.
Luke the doctor and budding writer added
the verbal frills that Renaissance painters
inserted later as white lily, blue anemone.
No realistic panty or split condom for them.
What an alibi! They were after the heavenly,
the paradox in straw. Thus, the lowly stall
for a king, the Magis' quest (those Romantics!)—
the *blaue Blume* found in a forest of hardships,
the wonder in a desert of distrust which was,
compared to making a virgin, an outcome
far beyond the storyteller's comprehension:
That his beautiful winged being, excited,
aroused, all muster, fluttering in pen and ink,
could infuse an old, wretched world with love.

WHERE IN THE WORLD
IS DIETERICH BUXTEHUDE?

After the investment in a day's minutiae
and obedience to their little must's and now's,
comes the enchantment of perfect music,
when over, the ultimate vanishing-act,
but while in our ears, a history of how one
then two or more guests become a world.
Humans are, in the end, strange animals
snuffling over bones we can't live without.

Come evening I want some Buxtehuda
around for company, some *Abendmusik*.
'Ah-behnt,' a word as beautiful as 'afternoon.'
Clouds roll off to wherever they're stored.
Old fellow of a moon comes out to top things off.
The grass, green without a summer's harshness.

Under Oxycodone's Wand

Need ice! The nurse's cupful ///oh, tinkling
of ice at breakfast ///has nothing to do
with a cocktail ///chatter away, distraction ///

amazing cloying. ///Females are so good at it ///
after 10,000 years of jello /// when you're good
to go home, you leave. /// I'll go check. OK. ///

They're not hers. So they're yours. Where're ///
my pants? You don't get those until you can walk. ///
I must try ///not to OD or they'll keep me. Longer.

*

White star there above my pillow, glaring down. //
Go away. Follow the moon. // The first magi //
wheels into my room riding a camel bearing

an odor of rotten myrrh. // It's the green robe
he's wearing. //Not for me. Leave I say. "Why?"
Why? // "Are you sure?" "Call the cops!" In the hall,

in the wilderness // women come rustling.
"Sh sh sh sh sh. Why say that? You've a nice
room here and meals. And us to look after you."

*

Out of the cradle, gently rocking, a shambles
for a floor. A slumber party? //Three pillows fly
through the air. All the aides are invited over

the intercom. //Take the bed apart, the extra blanket,
my pneumatic leg pumps. //They're baseball bases?
No, stage markers. //A smiling aide stands on them.

"Don't worry," she sings, "Be happy." / It's the only
English she and I know. Just her flowery voice /
and mine in this room. "Be happy," we croon.

*

I am a mole. I'm a muskrat lounging in the sun.
My remove is open, sunny and airy and free.
I've found the door to a secret garden. I can

sit at the patio table. Raise my face to sunlight.
Cuddle up to my winter coat. Down the street
a smoker's on the corner. I almost don't mind him.

So what if the table's gated, if the patio's patrolled
by an iron spear fence. Locked in. For one
fine hour I've come out of a hole into daylight.

*

Menea stands before me laying down the rules.
She puffs words through her pretty red lips.
Her bosom works in cahoots with her lungs. Up

and down. *I'm going home, Menea.* She
waves that aside, a familiar ranting. She
won't be the one to help me. *Jesus Savior,*

pilot me. Christian's voice is as deep
as he is tall. He rounds the room with pills,
a spell that can put a patient to sleep.

*

This is rehab for the repaired, the trapped.
Where's the door, the exit, the Orpheus who
wants to return the lame to upper world light?

She, my guide in a taupe hjjab, slips around
a hallway corner just when I thirst for help.
Tall, slender, and badged, she is the one

who leads me through the hallways' maze.
She who best understands longing? She says
the magic words–the outer door swings open.

CROSSING THE RIVER

The ferry is busy. An oily odor
greets us. And then our car

rolls on and we're crossing the river,
turbines churning like fever,

a queasy feeling, leaving green
summer behind. A funny thing,

you get used to low chatter,
the louder river and the motors.

The ferryman's an old timer,
a stout heart who delivers

his passengers to the shore
on the other side. In all these years

he's never had a casualty.
He's never had a stowaway.

REEDS, TOO,

in the topographical liturgy of northern Greece: Wooded mountains, lanes shaded by plane trees, sheep on hillsides, olive groves, vineyards, wheat fields suffering wild poppies' red gossip, small lakes, fishing skiffs, fishers waiting patiently over four thousand years for a nibble. The air smells sweet as Russian olive trees in spring. And if you're like me, from the Northern Plains, you'll notice the little tractors. By law they're little. What a shame if a big tractor's discs unearthed and squashed a golden cup, a black amphora, a bowl, a vase—ogled Thracian art that once thrived in the upper, air-world ruled by Alexander the Great, the handsome Macedonian driving his ten-horse-team-drawn gold carriage through cheering crowds. According to Diodorus, "...the people came out to meet it, and followed beside it when it went away, never wearied of their pleasure in the sight." Were you there? Yes? No? He'd have conquered you, too.

RE THE ART OF PAINTING/ DE SCHILDERKONST 1666-68/ JAN VERMEER

Wanting at least two sets of eyes, his
and his reflection's, Vermeer
devised contraptions
          like mirrors
for a better view
      of himself—

broad back and billowing bottom—
           in a room
where a huge wall map
      is a link
          to the North Sea.

De Noord See. The world. Its ships,

big as bugs
        where he, or I, on deck
could look out
      through imagination's
spyglass
        and see, really

see the only thing alive
          that counts
on a perfect June evening
is gathering
      surface & light
        and longing
and introduce them
     like destined lovers
       to each other.

On Good Wine Spilled

– after J.S. Bach, a 1748 letter

Because its cask cracked open, wagoned
as it was from Frankenland's vineyards
to raw, Baltic regions, the wine arrived
two thirds gone Bach immediately reported,
writing to his cousin, a loss to be mourned,
for the Lord Himself had dipped His finger
into its mellifluence, showing His preference
for trumpet blast and cymbal bong, for tongue
as messenger of new ideas or old ones
refurbished in glorious volume on an organ
of thanksgiving. What undervalued musician
would refrain from importuning a cousin for more?
(Bach volunteered to pay customs at the border.)
The wine glass stood near the composer's hand,
empty but ready to resume serious portions.

End of Winter

Suddenly magic in the crab apple tree's blueprint of sticks–
twenty-one robins, five waxwings and a pine finch

helicopter in, marauders in a rite of late
winter siege, a feasting called staying alive.

Bawdy and lusty and hungry and horny
probably, they barge into the tree's wattled rooms,

plucking and nipping apples, nudging and
warming their bellies on withered gelid flesh

as if the tree were an old madam's brothel.
I counted them more than once, in all,

twenty-seven birds, full of banter. The tree
did not let them leave as famished virgins.

THREE BISON

About their snow-speckled heads and legs:
in imitation a dancer dots his face white.
An artist paints a white and brown winter.

About their horns:
envious, an egotist adds to the centuries' closets
crowns, wreathes, miters, head dress.

The slaughterer admires how a horn rips through
hide and flesh, how hard his own blade
must drive to reach a bison's gut.

About the hidden stomach, like the aurochs'
40,000 years ago: it hungers for the wild
grasses sprouting under snow, under hoofs.

The waiting, the plodding across clearings,
the fear of slaughterers, of blood: What
I, too, know of hunger and thirst and longing.

T H Y M E

Old, single-syllable word with an old-fashioned *TH*
beginning, an ancient consonant-compound that lodges
back of front teeth and turns an *H* under tongue-pressure
into common *ta* to usher out a quaint *Υ*, sounding just like
long *i* today.—A trick older than a hand-made lace collar
that startles the dark bodice it circles. Elegant in form, *Υ*
is as totally at home mid-word as a tool in its chest. And
neighbor to *M*, a favorite human sound which floats away
with the silent *E*. A miracle the *E* hasn't been dropped;
it's a gnomic little happiness defending the presence of the
useless. A tale in nothingness. Whether recognized or not,
the *E* hangs on for dear life. Inaudible as fragrance. Maybe
carrying an important message from silence.

VESPERS

The censer swung like time shift, if time had legs,
joggling right to left in bursts of spicy fragrance,
flowery in honor of the pregnant Queen of Heaven,
her belly a globe, her breasts, milky knolls.

Continuity was a little group of believers
singing the same story this time each year
over two thousand years, the new version
wonderfully old on this late afternoon.

This as in two years ago or five hundred.
late as in tones clustering like supplicants.
afternoon as in the way a woman picks up her house

after company leaves, and ancient time
slowly squeezes into a new year.—The church door,
a gate pushed open from the outside to the inside dream.

LITTLE ETERNITIES

An energetic but murky mating in the bog—
frogs thick in the muck, no leg-room between,

not like patio chairs arranged to stand
apart from each other, not like families

separated by miles or rage, not like ghosts
of those long gone, rather like crowding

into a blinding urge to dwell intensely.
Look at shimmering leaves in sunlight,

they never move alone. Unless you remember
autumn's last leaf dangling on a branch.

But you won't, in spring you won't favor
a clan of faded ladies. I, too, dead-head

flowers to abet the next blossom.—Once
I walked in a field of peonies, of every color

and shirred petal. Blue dragonflies also visited.
The rain had stopped and the sun hadn't yet

unleashed its strongest beat. Thus around noon
for long moments, we were all together.

Note to the Reader: Imagination 'sometimes' stretches a word's history, but the impetus for writing the prose poems with one-word titles in *little eternities* sprang from reading *Word Origins* by Anatoly Liberman (Oxford University Press, 2005), an absolutely reliable source. Most of my title-words were in use between 900 to 1350 c.e.; the most recent to appear in print, *pummel*, dates from 1540. In *Poetry* (Oct. 2015, Vol. 207, Number 1), Ange Mlinko wrote, "Language itself is a character in the story, perhaps the closest thing we have to an omniscient one, containing all time and history, obfuscating and revealing at whim." Ergo the fun here in taking off on a word and following the subconscious or character wherever it leads.

Deepest thanks to the many poet friends and editors and Nodin Press who've helped me and all these poems on our way.

ACKNOWLEDGMENTS

The following poems have been published as they are in this book or in similar versions and/or under different names.

"Fragments from a Polish Journal,1889," "An Afternoon Spent Reading Madame Bovary": *Askew*

"Tea and Kippers," "Wretch," "Thyme": *Pirene's Fountain*

"The Village Bakery," "Chapel on the Mountain": *Solo Novo*

"Van Gogh Appears at the Café Amoré": *St. Paul Almanac*

"A Strange Falling": *Southern Humanities Review*

Third Section of "Time and Its Progress": *Evening Street Review*

"On Infusion," "On Good Wine Spilled": *Alehouse*

"I Won't Turn on the Radio": *Ascent*

"On Milton's Political Pampletts and the Measure of Time": *Epoch*

"Starry Nights of Pantry Labor," "On Time and Its Progress": *Contemporary American Voices*

"In Praise of Pencils": *Poetry East*

"Big," "These Old Women," "A White Rose Would Do…": *Pasque Petals*

"Crossing the River," "A Life with the Movies," "The Tsarina's Tea Set": *Whistling Shade*

"End of Winter": *Talking Stick*

"Re The Art of Painting/ De Schilderkonst": *Louisiana Literature*

"The Wounded Angel": *Commonweal*

"City of Arhirit": *Ekphrasis*

"Vespers," "Three Bison": *BoomerLitMag* (on line)

"Bilge," "Happiness": forthcoming in *Conduit*

Sharon Chmielarz was born and raised in Mobridge, South Dakota, but has spent her adult life in Minnesota. Her book *The Other Mozart*, a biography in poetry, was made into an opera. Her collection *Visibility: Ten Miles* was a finalist for the 2015 Midwest Book Awards, and *The Widow's House* was a finalist for the Next Generation Indie Book Awards and was named by *Kirkus Reviews* one of the best 100 books of 2016.

Chmielarz's work has been a finalist in the National Poetry Series, and her poems have been nominated several times for a Pushcart Prize. They have been featured on American Life in Poetry, and individual poems have been translated into French and Polish. She's the recipient of a Jane Kenyon Award from *The Water~Stone Review*. Her poems have been published in *The Notre Dame Review, The Iowa Review, Prairie Schooner, The Hudson Review, The North American Review, North Dakota Quarterly, Commonweal, Salmagundi, Margie, Salmagundi, The Seneca Review, Louisiana Literature, Ontario Review, CutBank,* and in Nodin Press's 2015 poetry anthology.